Agatha

Andrew

Greenway Quay
n the River Dart,
where Agatha
Christie owned
property.

Agatha Christie's novels and collections of short stories (translated into all the world's major languages) have recorded sales in excess of two billion copies, topped only by those of the Bible and Shakespeare. Her detective characters are famous throughout the world and have achieved the status of super sleuths.

But what of Agatha herself, their creator, the brains behind the legendary M. Hercule Poirot and Miss Jane Marple?

Agatha was a quiet, self-contained and retiring person who shunned publicity and rarely gave an interview, and therefore discovering the real Agatha is a challenging but by no means impossible task, worthy of her very own detectives. Fortunately, clues vital to the unravelling of the mystery of the author herself are to be found in her writings, and in particular in the novels which she wrote under the pseudonym 'Mary Westmacott'.

The Early Years

BELOW: Torquay, Agatha Christie's home town.

Agatha's parents were Clarissa (Clara), whose family came from Sussex, and Frederick Alvah Miller, an American who had moved to Manchester. The couple set up home in the Devonshire seaside resort of Torquay, at a house called 'Ashfield': 'a large villa with extensive gardens, an orchard, conservatories, a tennis court, and croquet lawn'. They were to have three children: Margaret (Madge), born in 1879; Louis Montant (Monty), born in 1880; and Agatha Mary Clarissa, who arrived on 15 September 1890.

Agatha describes her mother as imaginative, creative, highly intuitive and somewhat melodramatic. Her father, she says, was a lazy man of independent means; a collector of fine furniture and china, glass and paintings, who spent mornings and afternoons at his club and, during the season, days at the cricket club. He possessed an extensive library, which was of benefit to Agatha as her literary career blossomed.

As a young girl she was devoted to her nanny – 'Nursie' – and when she retired Agatha described this as the 'first real sorrow of my life'. There was also a cook, housemaids and a parlour maid. But in this seemingly perfect world all was not well, for when Agatha was about five years old her father began to experience financial difficulties.

The Millers let Ashfield to spend the winter of 1895 in France, where the cost of living was lower. Here Agatha, with the help of Marie Sijé – an assistant they met in a dressmaker's shop – soon become fluent in French. When the family returned to England, Marie accompanied them as Agatha's governess.

Agatha was lonely as a child, partly because her siblings were a decade older than she was, but also because her mother would not allow her to attend school. This loneliness was exacerbated when Nursie retired and Marie Sijé returned to France after three years with the family. That her sheltered upbringing failed to prepare her for the rough and tumble of adult life was a fact about which Agatha would later complain bitterly. On the other hand, had she not been lonely then perhaps she would not have developed that wonderful imagination with which she entertained herself, and which she would one day use to the full when embarking on her writing career.

Although Agatha learned to read at an early age, she also loved to hear stories. Madge introduced her to Sherlock Holmes and Agatha so enjoyed *The Levenworth Case* that she pestered her sister to read her more of his adventures. She was fascinated, too, by accounts of real-life criminal trials which she read about in newspapers.

In order to compensate for her loneliness, Agatha invented a circle of imaginary playmates for herself, including 'Lord Tony', based on the Yorkshire terrier given to her as a puppy on her fifth birthday – a gift which gave her 'unimaginable joy'.

By Agatha's early teens her mother was a widow, Frederick Miller having died in 1901. Clara decided that Agatha should attend a school for girls in Torquay and, a year later, she was sent to a school in Paris, then to a finishing school. Agatha described the time spent in the French capital as amongst the happiest days she had ever known; at long last, she could enjoy the company of people her own age.

In her autobiography Agatha suggests that she enjoyed being frightened. She describes a terrifying game she and Madge played called 'The Elder Sister': a reference to an imaginary sibling, senior to Madge and herself, who was mad and lived in a cave. Although Agatha experienced 'indescribable terror' when this game was played, she confessed it was always initiated by her.

This desire to play such a frightening game is perhaps surprising as from the age of four young Agatha experienced bad dreams, as many children do. Hers centred around someone she called 'The Gunman', who she described as a Frenchman with powdered hair in a pigtail, dressed in uniform and bearing a musket. She would be dreaming, say, of enjoying a tea party, a walk with her family or a festive occasion, when she would be overcome with a feeling of uneasiness, that there was someone present 'who ought not to be there'. This feeling quickly gave way to 'a horrid feeling of fear ... His pale-blue eyes would meet mine, and I would wake up shrieking, "The Gunman, The Gunman!"'.

A sense of anxiety was to become a part of Agatha's make up: she feared change, losing her home and – more importantly – being separated from her loved ones. This was to have consequences on her future well-being, as will be seen later when the idyllic world for which she always longed fell apart.

Writing, Romance and War

Did Agatha always intend to be a writer? The answer is no, because in her youth her main preoccupation was with music and drama. However, the instinct to write was present within her from an early age.

She describes her first attempts at poetry as 'unbelievably awful', but persevered and duly appeared in print at the age of 11. By her late teens she had won several prizes and some of her poems were printed in *The Poetry Review*. She then went through a phase of being 'addicted to writing psychic stories' before declaring that her only ambition for the future was to have 'a happy marriage'.

A bored Agatha was convalescing from influenza when her mother suggested that she attempt to write a story. 'The House of Beauty' was the result, and several others followed – all typed by Agatha on her sister's Empire typewriter. They were sent off to various magazines, but without success.

When Agatha decided she would like to try writing a detective story, Madge declared that such a project would prove too difficult. From that time Agatha 'was fired by a determination' to prove her sibling wrong.

Madge had married in 1902; her younger sister always looked forward to the day she too would marry, and as a young woman had several suitors. In fact Agatha was engaged to another when she met her future husband – Archie Christie – at a dance. It was 12 October 1912. She was aged 22 and Archie, an Army officer awaiting admission to the newly created Royal Flying Corps (RFC), was 23.

In Agatha's early life her brother Monty played a lesser role than Madge as he was often far from home. When the Boer War broke out in 1899 he volunteered; when the war ended in 1902 he obtained a commission in the East Surrey Regiment, leaving South Africa for India. He rejoined the Army at the commencement of the First World War in 1914.

ABOVE: Fruits from various species of strychnine tree, including strychnos toxifera – source of the poison curare – and strychnos nux-vomica – source of the poison known as strychnine.

ABOVE: Agatha and her husband Archie Christie in 1919.

Early in 1914, Agatha studied for an examination in First Aid and Home Nursing, spending two mornings per week at Torquay Hospital's Out-patients' Department and a further day with the district nurse. She then joined the Voluntary Aid Detachment.

Following the outbreak of war on 4 August 1914, the first casualties began arriving at Torquay railway station, to be taken to an improvised 'hospital' – the converted Town Hall – where Agatha was working as a nursing auxiliary. She later declared that, had she not married, she would have 'trained as a real hospital nurse'. On 5 August, Archie, to whom she was now engaged, left for France with the British Expeditionary Force.

At Christmastime 1914 Archie came home on leave, and he and Agatha were married on Christmas Eve. They spent a brief honeymoon at Torquay's Grand Hotel, Christmas Day with Agatha's mother and, on Boxing Day, the newly-weds travelled to London and said farewell as he left, once more, for France.

During the war Archie displayed conspicuous bravery, being mentioned several times in dispatches and decorated. His days of active flying, however, came to an end in the summer of 1915, owing to a sinus condition.

Later that year Agatha commenced work at Torquay Hospital's dispensary, where she studied for the Apothecaries Hall Examination. At that time pharmacists were governed by the Poisons and Pharmacy Act of 1908, where virtually all substances which would now be called 'medicines' were classed as 'poisons'. Agatha subsequently composed a poem entitled 'In a Dispensary', featuring poisons such as monkshood blue, aconite and deadly cyanide.

One day the pharmacist, whom Agatha referred to as 'Mr P', removed from his pocket 'a dark coloured lump'. He told her that it was curare: a substance which, when taken by mouth, was entirely harmless; however, should it enter the bloodstream it would first paralyse and then kill. It was used as an arrow poison. So why did he choose to keep it in his pocket? Because, he said, it made him feel powerful.

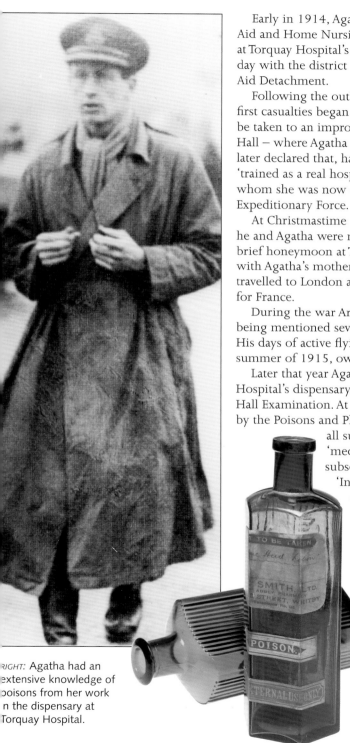

RIGHT: Agatha had an extensive knowledge of poisons from her work in the dispensary at Torquay Hospital.

Writing, Romance and War

BELOW: David Suchet as Hercule Poirot, the retired Belgian policeman turned private detective who appeared in Agatha's first crime novel.

The effect of this statement on the young Agatha, whose mind was bursting with the adventures of the fictional Sherlock Holmes and real-life murder trials, may be imagined – for it was while she was working in the dispensary that she first conceived the idea of writing a detective story. 'Since I was surrounded by poisons, perhaps it was natural that death by poisoning should be the method I selected,' she said.

As for her detective, Agatha was determined that he should be quite distinct from others such as Sherlock Holmes. She decided to make him a Belgian, there being a number of Belgian war refugees resident in her local parish of Torre. A retired chief of the Belgian Police Force, he would be tidy in his habits and very brainy – the possessor of an abundance of the 'little grey cells of the mind'. Finally, she settled on his name: Hercule Poirot.

When the intricacies of the plot began to get the better of her, Clara advised her daughter to go on holiday in order to concentrate. So it was that in the summer of 1916 Agatha spent a fortnight at the Moorland Hotel on Dartmoor where she completed her book, *The Mysterious Affair at Styles*.

After rejections from two other publishers, Agatha sent her manuscript to Bodley Head, who promptly 'forgot all about it'. They later agreed to publish it – but only after considerable changes were made. It was not, therefore, until December 1920 that it was published – first in America and a month later in England.

ABOVE: *The Mysterious Affair at Styles*, Agatha Christie's first crime novel, sold for 7 shillings and 6 pence (35p) when it was published in London in 1921.

Marriage and Motherhood

ABOVE: Agatha with her daughter Rosalind, *c.*1924.

When Archie was posted to the Air Ministry in London in the summer of 1918, the couple set up home in the capital in a rented flat. Agatha commenced a study of bookkeeping and shorthand, but confessed, once again, to being lonely. She missed the hospital, the friends she had made there and the day-to-day routine. She also missed Ashfield, the family home.

By the end of the First World War, Archie had reached the rank of colonel at the young age of 29. After the signing of the Armistice on 11 November 1918 he came home on leave, during which time Agatha discovered she was pregnant.

Agatha's priority had always been to achieve a happy marriage and now she had a dashing, masterful and exciting husband with whom she wanted to create a happy and loving home for their forthcoming child: a child who would be loved and cherished, just as her own parents had loved and cherished her. On 5 August 1919, Agatha gave birth to a daughter, Rosalind. The odds of her having a happy marriage and a happy life appeared to be greatly in her favour. Or were they?

Sadly, even at this early stage of her marriage, there were signs that Agatha was not entirely happy. With Archie's increasing dedication to golf, she found herself spending every weekend at the golf course at East Croydon, which was not to her liking. She would have much preferred to visit new places or go for long walks in the countryside.

When she voiced her concerns about the expense of maintaining Ashfield, Archie suggested that her mother might sell the house and make her home elsewhere. Agatha was against this idea, but agreed with his alternative suggestion – that she write another book and thereby raise funds to assist her mother. This she duly did, also supplementing her income by having her work serialized in *The Weekly Times*.

Scenes and Settings

Agatha was particularly fond of dogs and is seen here with her pet, c.1920.

As with many writers, Agatha's life experiences feature in her work, both in respect of what she loved – such as dogs and trains – as well as places and things she had knowledge of – such as poison and golf. It is no surprise, therefore, that with a husband who had served in the Royal Flying Corps, Agatha wrote a novel relating to aircraft: *Death in the Clouds*.

In her novel *Dead Man's Folly*, her home town of Torquay appears under its own name. *The Sittaford Mystery* is set in one of her favourite places – Dartmoor. In *Peril at End House*, although Agatha speaks of the Cornish coast there is little doubt that she is thinking of her home county of Devon: St Loo being Torquay and the Majestic Hotel being based on the real-life Imperial Hotel.

Although Agatha was in no way as enthusiastic about golf as Archie, she was a proficient player. In *Murder in the Mews*, Mrs Barbara Allen is found dead in her apartment with a pistol in her right hand. Poirot notices that the murdered woman's golf clubs are for someone who is left-handed, which has a significant bearing on the case.

BURGH ISLAND

One of Agatha's favourite locations was the 28-acre Burgh Island, situated offshore from the resort of Bigbury-on-Sea on the South Devon coast. It is separated from the mainland by a sand bar, across which a passenger-carrying 'sea tractor' can operate in up to six feet of water, in all but the roughest conditions. Burgh Island was purchased in 1929 by millionaire Archibald Nettlefold who built a luxurious art deco hotel there, which provided the inspiration for two Agatha Christie novels: *And Then There Were None* and *Evil under the Sun*.

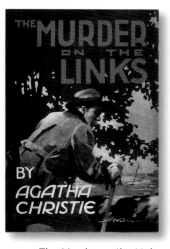

ABOVE: Death in the Clouds was published in 1935 and described by *The New York Times* as 'a crime puzzle of first quality and mighty entertaining story besides'.

ABOVE: The Murder on the Links, first published in 1923; Agatha herself was an experienced and proficient golfer, and won a handicap competition.

ABOVE: Colonel Archie Christie, Agatha's first husband, in flying gear; he was in the RFC during the First World War.

LEFT: Burgh Island, a one-time haunt of smugglers and a source of inspiration for Agatha Christie.

In *Why Didn't They Ask Evans?* Bobby Jones is playing golf when he drives his ball over the edge of a cliff. In going to retrieve it, he discovers a man has been deliberately pushed to his death. *The Murder on the Links*, however, has very little to do with golf, apart from a body being found on the golf course at a proposed site for what Poirot refers to as a 'bunkire' – which he charmingly defines as 'the irregular hole filled with sand and a bank at one side, is it not?'

Agatha was particularly attached to her dogs and they too found their way into her stories. The appropriately named *Dumb Witness*, for example, features a wire-haired terrier called Bob, about which Agatha writes in glowing terms.

Until she had her first motor car in her 30s, Agatha depended greatly on trains for travelling. 'Trains are wonderful; I still adore them,' she said. This mode of transport was to appear in many of her stories, including *4.50 from Paddington* and *The ABC Murders*.

Literary Success, Problems – and a Mystery

'Two summits of ambition fulfilled: dining with the Queen of England; and the proud ownership of a bottle-nosed Morris – a car of my own!'

AGATHA CHRISTIE: AN AUTOBIOGRAPHY

With her increasing literary success, Agatha was able, at Archie's suggestion, to purchase a Morris Cowley motor car. To drive it gave her enormous pleasure. By now, the realization was beginning that perhaps one day she might become a writer by profession, though she was disappointed at what she perceived to be a lack of encouragement from Archie.

The couple lived in Sunningdale, Berkshire, and it was here in 1925 that they bought their first house, 'Styles', named after Agatha's first book, *The Mysterious Affair at Styles*. She hoped to have another baby but Rosalind was to remain an only child.

Agatha's mother died at the age of 72 in 1926. Archie was in Spain and unable to be present at the funeral, and when he returned to England he stayed at his London club while Agatha was at Ashfield sorting out her mother's belongings. She could not bear to part with the house so decided to let it.

Agatha's feelings at this time are mirrored in her semi-autobiographical novel *Unfinished Portrait* (published in 1934 under the pseudonym 'Mary Westmacott'); the sentiments expressed throughout the book reveal her unhappiness. In the story Celia (Agatha's counterpart) describes her husband Dermot as being a person incapable of empathizing with the 'emotional stress' of others.

ABOVE: Agatha's abandoned motor car, discovered on 4 December 1926 at Newlands Corner, Guildford, Surrey.

RIGHT: 'Styles' in Sunningdale, the Berkshire home purchased by Agatha and Archie in the 1920s.

On 3 December 1926, Agatha, now aged 36, disappeared for 11 days – her whereabouts unknown, despite a nationwide police search. The event caused considerable interest and gave rise to much speculation. The world's most famous mystery writer had herself become the subject of mystery.

The day after her disappearance, her motor car was discovered on a slope near a chalk pit in a remote lane in Surrey, 12 miles from her home. What could have possessed her to abandon her precious Morris Cowley, her pride and joy?

It was not until Tuesday 14 December that her whereabouts finally became known – thanks to two observant musicians who worked at the Hydropathic Hotel ('The Hydro') in Harrogate, Yorkshire.

When Archie travelled to meet Agatha at The Hydro on 14 December, he was due for a shock. The event was reported by the *Harrogate Advertiser*: 'He [Archie] went up and spoke to her [Agatha], but she did not recognize him as her husband. She turned to some fellow guests and said, "I am excited because my brother has arrived."'

But this was only part of the story, for it transpired that from the time Agatha had arrived at The Hydro she had behaved in a most extraordinary manner. Said the *Harrogate Advertiser*: 'The lady in question arrived at the Harrogate Hydro on Saturday night, December 4th, and had with her only an attaché case. She registered under the name of Mrs Teresa Neele, and was understood to have come from the Cape Colony.'

ABOVE: *Unfinished Portrait*, the semi-autobiographical novel reflecting a period of great unhappiness in Agatha's life.

Literary Success, Problems – and a Mystery

NOTED JOCKEY KILLED IN A MOTORING ACCIDENT

Daily Mirror

MAJOR BLAKE FINED £250

THE DAILY PICTURE   NEWSPAPER WITH THE LARGEST NET SALE

No. 7,207   THURSDAY, DECEMBER 16, 1926   One Penny

MRS. CHRISTIE'S DRAMATIC DASH TO SECLUSION

ABOVE: The author's mysterious disappearance and subsequent discovery made the headlines in all the national newspapers.

Furthermore, on Saturday 11 December, an advertisement had appeared in *The Times*, placed by Agatha herself, which suggests that she was suffering from some sort of identity crisis:

FRIENDS and RELATIVES of TERESA NEELE, late of South Africa, COMMUNICATE. Write Box R.702, The Times, E.C.4.

Agatha's account of events, given over a year later to the *Daily Mail*, confirms that she did indeed experience a change of identity, for as she herself stated, up to the moment of her car leaving the road, 'I was Mrs Christie', whereas on her arrival at The Hydro, 'I had now become in my mind Mrs Teresa Neele of South Africa.'

Although Agatha may have been temporarily dazed when her car ran off the road, this does not explain her subsequent behaviour. In her distressed state Agatha recognized neither herself (even when she saw her own photograph in the newspapers of the day, which were reporting on the continuing search for her), nor her daughter (whose photograph she carried with her and whom she mistook for a son), nor her family or friends.

Was it a coincidence that she chose the name 'Neele' for her metamorphosis? It seems not, for this was the name of the woman with whom her husband Archie was having an affair.

In *Unfinished Portrait*, where Agatha relives her experience vicariously through 'Celia', the latter flees from her home in desperation and forgets her late mother's name and her own identity. And just as the fictional 'Larraby' helps Celia to resolve her emotional difficulties, so a real-life doctor, Geoffrey Lucas of Norfolk, whom Agatha met in the Canary Islands in 1927, helped her in a similar way, advising that whatever the future may hold she must 'accept it and go on'.

In April 1928 Agatha and Archie were granted a decree nisi, and on 29 October of that year the couple's divorce was finalized. Eighteen days later, on 16 November, Archie married Nancy Neele.

Tradition and Characters

Despite all the upheavals in her life, Agatha's writing continued unabated, with a total of 11 major novels and short-story collections published in the 1920s. However, to say that she was driven by some kind of work ethic would be untrue. She could never understand why people tended to assume that there was 'something meritorious about working'. She simply saw it as a way of earning money.

She did not find writing new novels easy, but laboured to bring into her stories the detail of everyday things that were important to her. She shared with her fictional detective Miss Marple a love of tradition and a dislike of change: the inundation of every village and hamlet by people who had no ties or kinship with those already there; the way that country cottages were being converted for the use of newcomers, so that nobody actually knew anymore who anybody was.

RIGHT: Hercule Poirot with his assistant Captain Hastings in *Lord Edgware Dies*, from the award-winning television series *Poirot*.

CHRISTIE CHARACTERS

As well as the more famous M. Poirot and Miss Marple, other notable characters from Agatha Christie's pen include: Tommy and Tuppence Beresford, who founded the Young Adventurers Ltd and embark on a life of crime-solving together; Mr Satterthwaite, friend of Hercule Poirot, whose associate Harley Quin possesses magical powers which he uses to prevent evil from occurring; Chief Inspector James Japp of Scotland Yard, who features in many of Poirot's most famous cases; Colonel Lucius Protheroe of Old Hall, St Mary Mead, who is found dead at the vicarage; Ariadne Oliver, writer of detective novels and friend of and assistant to Poirot; and Christopher Parker Pyne – another sleuth, though less energetic than Poirot.

Tradition and Characters

Agatha loved so much of what, in her time, was regarded as being quintessentially English – village life, steam trains, correct etiquette and good manners. And yet, having travelled widely and lived abroad, she, with her keen sense of humour, was able to see the English as others see them, and poke gentle fun at such English qualities as reticence, distrust of foreigners and sangfroid.

Agatha's lifelong love of flowers – one of her earliest memories was of mauve irises on the wallpaper in her nursery – became a feature of many of her books: in *At Bertram's Hotel*, Miss Marple describes the rose-patterned wallpaper in her bedroom; and the opening words of *The Body in the Library* read 'Mrs Bantry was dreaming. Her sweet peas had just taken a First at the flower show.'

RIGHT: Joan Hickson as Miss Marple, Agatha Christie's most famous female sleuth.

BELOW: The Murder at the Vicarage (1930), the first novel to feature Miss Marple. Jane Marple was based on spinster Caroline Sheppard who appeared in *The Murder of Roger Ackroyd* (1926).

MISS JANE MARPLE

Of female detectives Jane Marple, an elderly spinster, is unquestionably the First Lady. She lives in the fictitious village of St Mary Mead, which she regards as a microcosm of the world at large, and makes her first appearance in a short story entitled *The Tuesday Night Club*. Her technique is to see without being seen, to regard everyone as a suspect and not to believe everything that people tell her.

'Oh, I'm sure you're far too busy to listen to my little ideas.'
MISS MARPLE TO INSPECTOR SLACK IN *THE MURDER AT THE VICARAGE*

LEFT: Peter Ustinov as Poirot in the 1982 film *Evil Under the Sun*; the book of the same name was published in 1941.

BELOW: Nether Wallop in Hampshire: the setting for the fictional village of St Mary Mead in the television drama *Miss Marple* in which Joan Hickson played the title role.

And so it is that in Agatha's writings one can almost smell the roses in Miss Marple's garden; hear the buzzing of bees; the rustle of her housemaid's dress as she brings out the tea tray; the church clock striking the hour; the errand boy whistling as he rides by, his bicycle tyres crunching on the gravel path. What better devices could Agatha have employed to heighten the feeling of anticipation in her readers, who trust implicitly that she will not disappoint them, and that within a few turns of the page this sublime scene will be transformed by a murder most foul?

M. HERCULE POIROT

One of Agatha Christie's best-known characters, this former Belgian policeman is a dapper little man with an egg-shaped head who sports a moustache and a tiny pair of pince-nez. In 1916, during the First World War, he is forced to flee his native land and take up residence in England. Here, assisted by his friend and confidant Captain Arthur Hastings, he establishes himself as a private detective of considerable renown, his first case being *The Mysterious Affair at Styles*. In this story Emily Inglethorpe, who has provided accommodation for Belgian refugees of the war, is murdered, and Poirot is highly motivated to find her killer.

'These little grey cells. It is "up to them" – as you say over here.'
POIROT IN *THE MYSTERIOUS AFFAIR AT STYLES*

The Middle East – and a New Life

In the autumn of 1928 Agatha was invited to dine with friends in London, and a chance meeting with young naval officer Commander Howe – recently returned from the Middle East – changed her life forever.

Agatha, who 'had always been faintly attracted to archaeology, though knowing nothing about it', was already aware of the work of English archaeologist Leonard Woolley at Ur in Iraq. Having extolled the virtues of Baghdad, Commander Howe suggested that she might like to visit that city. Furthermore, she could travel there by train – in fact by none other than the *Orient Express*.

On Agatha's arrival in Iraq she met Woolley, whose wife, Katharine, arranged for her to visit the cities of Nejef and Kerbala, which had 'a wonderful mosque' with a gold and turquoise dome. On this excursion Agatha was escorted by Max Mallowan, who for the last five years had been Woolley's assistant. Despite Max being several years her junior, romance blossomed and on 11 September 1930 they were married in the chapel of St Columba's Church in Edinburgh.

Agatha took a keen interest in Max's work and was involved in excavations with him from 1930 to 1938. They would leave England for the Middle East around the turn of the year, returning in March after a season's digging. During this time Agatha's daughter, Rosalind, was at public school in Kent, but on one occasion joined her mother and stepfather on a dig in Syria.

BELOW: Agatha with second husband Max Mallowan, January 1946.

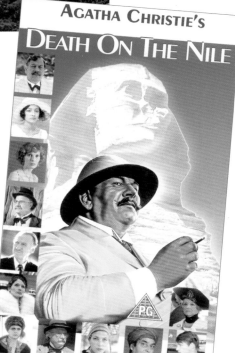

In the summer of 1938 Agatha and Max returned to England and set up home at No. 48 Sheffield Terrace, London. Agatha also purchased 'Greenway', a mansion dating from the reign of William and Mary, which stands in extensive grounds and overlooks South Devon's picturesque River Dart. This they used as a holiday home.

When the Second World War broke out, Max joined the Home Guard at Brixham, Devon, and Agatha volunteered to work, once again, in the dispensary at the hospital in Torquay. Soon afterwards, when Max joined the Air Ministry, she joined him in London and Greenway was let to a children's nursery from the capital. Greenway was subsequently requisitioned by the Admiralty and taken over by officers of the United States Navy.

From 1940 to 1945 Max served in the Royal Air Force Volunteer Reserve as Liaison Officer with Allied forces and as Civilian Affairs Officer in North Africa. Meanwhile, in 1941 Agatha's daughter married Hubert Prichard, a major in the regular Army; a son, Mathew, arrived in 1943. But in August 1944 Rosalind received a telegram to say that her husband had been killed in action in France.

The Middle East – and a New Life

When the war ended in 1945, Greenway was derequisitioned. In 1947 Max, now Professor of Western Asiatic Archaeology at London University, returned with Agatha to the Middle East after an absence of 10 years. As Director of Iraq's British School of Archaeology he organized a dig at Nimrud, one-time military capital of Assyria – a project that would take 12 years. Agatha was fascinated by the objects unearthed and in her element to be amongst people she considered friends, who were affectionate, unsophisticated and full of the joys of life. During this time, in 1949, Rosalind was remarried, to barrister Anthony Hicks.

After more than a decade of winters spent in the Middle East, Agatha – not surprisingly – based several of her written works in this region, for example: *Murder on the Orient Express* (published in 1934); *Murder in Mesopotamia* (1936); *Death on the Nile* (1937); *Death Comes as the End* (1945); and *Come, Tell Me How You Live* (1946).

ABOVE: Now in the British Museum, London, this Phoenician panel, dating from the 9th–8th century BC, was discovered by Max Mallowan at the Palace of Ashurnasirpal, Nimrud, Iraq.

GREENWAY

Greenway was the holiday home of Agatha and Max from 1938 until 1959 and proved to be the inspiration for *Dead Man's Folly* (first published in 1956) which features the boathouse here. Greenway itself was, said Agatha, 'A white Georgian house of about 1780 or 90, with woods sweeping down to the [River] Dart below, and a lot of fine shrubs and trees – the ideal house, a dream house.' Here she tended the garden, played her piano, and read, on summer evenings to family and friends from her latest thriller as they attempted to guess 'whodunit'!

In 1959 Greenway was transferred by Agatha to her daughter Rosalind, who, with her husband Anthony Hicks took up residence in 1968 and lived there until her death. In 2000 the family donated Greenway, together with its garden and Lower Greenway Farm, to the National Trust, and in 2006 a £5.4 million restoration of the house and collection began.

The Final Years

On 20 December 1962 Agatha's first husband, Archie, died aged 73. That same year she was invited to attend a party in London to celebrate the tenth anniversary of the opening of her play *The Mousetrap*. 'People like it, but who can say why?' she said in her typically modest way.

When in 1968 Max was knighted, Agatha became Lady Mallowan. In 1971, her 80th year, she was appointed Dame of the British Empire (DBE). In her lifetime Agatha's published works included 66 crime novels, 13 short-story collections, 15 plays, six other novels and an autobiography.

Agatha died, aged 85, on 12 January 1976 at Winterbrook House – the home in Wallingford (now in Oxfordshire) that she and Max had owned since 1934. They had been married for 45 years. On the day she died the lights of West End theatres were dimmed in her honour. She is buried in St Mary's Churchyard at Cholsey village, near Wallingford. On 13 May a memorial service was held for her at the London church of St Martin-in-the-Fields. Her autobiography was published posthumously the following year.

ABOVE: Agatha beside the River Thames in the grounds of Winterbrook House, Wallingford, 1950.

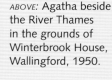

LEFT: A cake baked to celebrate the 50th anniversary of *The Mousetrap*, November 2002.

THE MOUSETRAP

Agatha Christie's *The Mousetrap* is the stage version of her radio play *Three Blind Mice*, written to celebrate Queen Mary's 80th birthday in 1947.

The Mousetrap – the copyright for which Agatha gifted to her only grandchild – began its West End run on 25 November 1952, and starred Richard Attenborough. As a result of the play's success, Agatha in 1965 donated £310,000 to the Harrison Homes for Elderly Ladies of Limited Means (of which there were 18 in the London suburbs of Kensington and Hammersmith), followed by further gifts totalling £50,000. Still running to this day, it is the longest running play of all time.

The Queen of Crime

Agatha began serious writing only when challenged by her sister to do so. When she discovered that she was good at it, she saw this not as a way of becoming famous but as a way of making the money which would enable her to fulfil her relatively modest needs. And when fame did come, she was bemused by it.

Miss Marple, Poirot and Agatha's other sleuths are all characters into whose lives we love to enter, and whom we admire for their dazzling brilliance. It is they whom we trust to unravel the mystery and bring the murderer to justice. However, when we attempt to solve the mystery ourselves we discover that there are many characters, all of whom, seemingly, have equal motive and opportunity to perform the dastardly deed. Yet we are challenged to attempt the solution, for we know that as often as not Agatha has cleverly presented us with all the necessary clues with which to do so.

Her characters are vividly portrayed, her plots are plausible and we are excited by the locations in which she chooses to stage them – whether this be Dartmoor, the Middle East, aboard the *Orient Express* or in the Caribbean – hence the enduring appeal of Agatha Christie's detective novels. She is truly 'the 'Queen of Crime'.

ABOVE: Agatha at work: Winterbrook House, Wallingford, 1950.

RIGHT: The 1974 film *Murder on the Orient Express* has an all-star cast which includes Vanessa Redgrave, Sean Connery, Ingrid Bergman, Albert Finney and Lauren Bacall.